KINGDOM CLASSIFICATION

FERNS, MOSSES & OTHER
SPORE-PRODUCING PLANTS

By Steve Parker

First published in the United States in 2009 by
Compass Point Books
151 Good Counsel Drive
P.O. Box 669
Mankato, MN 56002-0669

ANIMAL KINGDOM CLASSIFICATION—SPORE-PRODUCING
PLANTS was produced by

David West Children's Books
7 Princeton Court
55 Felsham Road
London SW15 1AZ

Designer: Rob Shone
Editors: Gail Bushnell, Anthony Wacholtz
Page Production: Bobbie Nuytten

Art Director: Joe Ewest
Creative Director: LuAnn Ascheman-Adams
Editorial Director: Nick Healy
Managing Editor: Catherine Neitge

Library of Congress Cataloging-in-Publication Data
Parker, Steve, 1952–
  Ferns, mosses & other spore-producing plants / by Steve
Parker.
     p. cm.—(Kingdom classifications)
  Includes index.
  ISBN 978-0-7565-4220-7 (library binding)
  1. Ferns—Juvenile literature. 2. Mosses—Juvenile literature.
3. Plant spores—Juvenile literature.
I. Title. II. Title: Ferns, mosses and other spore-producing
plants. III. Series: Parker, Steve, 1952– Kingdom
classifications.
  QK522.5.P37 2010
  587.3 dc22   2009012060

Visit Compass Point Books on the Internet at
www.compasspointbooks.com
or e-mail your request to
custserv@compasspointbooks.com

Front cover: Moss sporophytes
Opposite: Blechnaceae fiddlehead frond

KINGDOM CLASSIFICATION

FERNS, MOSSES & OTHER SPORE-PRODUCING PLANTS

Steve Parker

Compass Point Books ✦ Minneapolis, Minnesota

TABLE OF CONTENTS

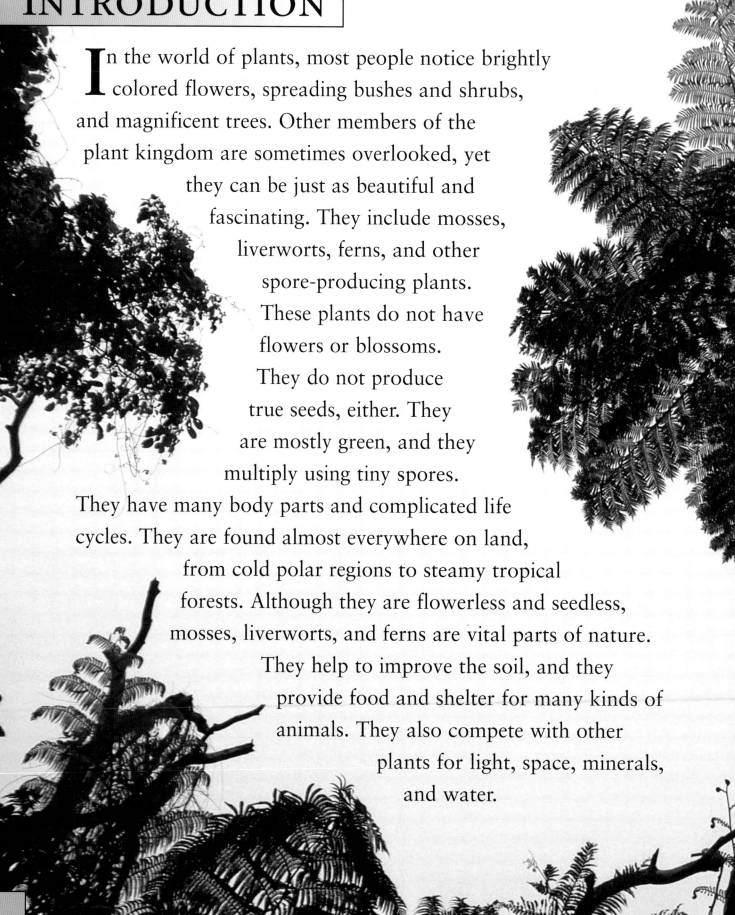

In the world of plants, most people notice brightly colored flowers, spreading bushes and shrubs, and magnificent trees. Other members of the plant kingdom are sometimes overlooked, yet they can be just as beautiful and fascinating. They include mosses, liverworts, ferns, and other spore-producing plants. These plants do not have flowers or blossoms. They do not produce true seeds, either. They are mostly green, and they multiply using tiny spores. They have many body parts and complicated life cycles. They are found almost everywhere on land, from cold polar regions to steamy tropical forests. Although they are flowerless and seedless, mosses, liverworts, and ferns are vital parts of nature. They help to improve the soil, and they provide food and shelter for many kinds of animals. They also compete with other plants for light, space, minerals, and water.

TALL AS A TREE

Not all mosses, liverworts, and ferns are small. Tree ferns resemble palm trees (which are flowering plants). But they are actually tall types of ferns with a single woody trunk and an umbrella-shaped crown of fronds. One of them, the Cyathea lepifera, *which lives in the mountains of East and Southeast Asia, can grow to be 20 feet (6 meters) tall.*

PLANTS, SPORES, AND SEEDS

Some groups of plants—the spermatophytes—have flowers and make seeds. But other groups, including mosses, liverworts, and ferns, do not.

REPRODUCTION

Mosses, liverworts, ferns, and their cousins reproduce by spores. A spore is usually a single microscopic cell in a tough, resistant casing. In general, spores are not made by sexual reproduction, which is the joining of gametes—female and male sex cells. Seeds differ because they are made from flowers by sexual reproduction, and each contains a baby plant called an embryo, with many cells.

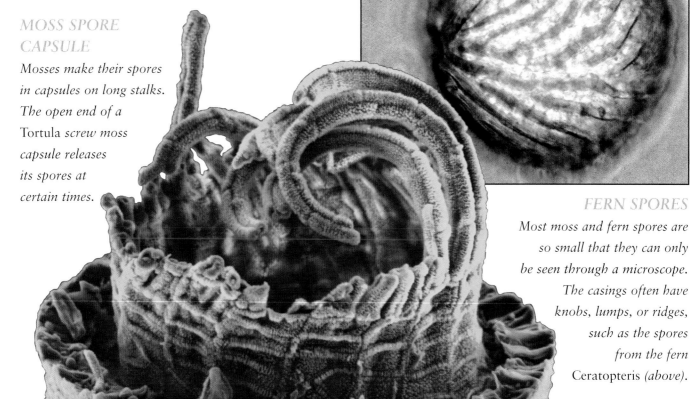

MOSS SPORE CAPSULE

Mosses make their spores in capsules on long stalks. The open end of a Tortula *screw moss capsule releases its spores at certain times.*

FERN SPORES

Most moss and fern spores are so small that they can only be seen through a microscope. The casings often have knobs, lumps, or ridges, such as the spores from the fern Ceratopteris *(above).*

POLLEN

Flowering plants begin reproduction by producing male sex cells in tiny pollen grains (left). These join with female egg cells to form the seeds.

SPREADING AROUND

The pollen grains and the seeds of flowering plants are spread by various means, such as the wind (above left), animals (above right), and water. The spores of mosses, liverworts, and ferns travel in similar ways.

SPORE GERMINATION

The spores from Polytrichum hair moss needs nutrients and moisture to grow.

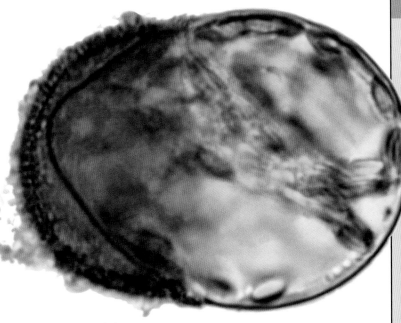

SMALL SPORES, BIG SEEDS

Typical moss spores are less than 0.0004 inch (0.01 millimeters) across. Most fern spores are not much bigger, perhaps 0.002 inch (0.05 mm), like very fine powder. In contrast, the largest flowering plant seed is the seed of the coco-de-mer, which is about 20 inches (50 centimeters) long.

The coco-de-mer is a seed-containing fruit of the Lodoicea palm tree.

DISPERSAL

Most spores do not reserve nutrients, as seeds do. Spores spread in water, on the wind, and on animals. This moves the spores away from the parent plant to new places. If the conditions are good, spores take in water and minerals from the surroundings and grow into new plants.

PREHISTORIC PLANTS

Ferns and their relatives were among the first large plants to appear on land many millions of years ago.

FOSSIL FERN

Ferns preserved as fossils from more than 100 million years ago (right) look similar to modern types (below).

SWAMP SCENE

During the Carboniferous period (299 million to 359 million years ago), giant dragonflies and early four-legged amphibians lived among the giant ferns.

FERN FROND

The main leaf of a fern is known as a frond or blade. The small dark spots on the frond are the spore-making capsules, called sporangia.

THE FIRST FERNS

Ferns, mosses, liverworts, and their cousins were growing on land long before flowering plants. Fossils are the remains of once-living things that were buried, preserved in the rocks, and turned to stone. Fossils of ferns date back to the Devonian period more than 360 million years ago. They were food for early land animals such as insects, millipedes, and amphibians. They also helped to make the soil, which was forming over the once-bare rocks.

THE GONDWANA TREE

Glossopteris (Gondwana tree) was a widespread, treelike seed fern—a now extinct group of ferns that made seeds. It grew when the southern continents were joined as one landmass, Gondwana.

A fossil of Glossopteris from 220 million years ago was recently found in Antarctica.

CALAMITES

Horsetails (bottom) are closely related to ferns. Long ago they were much larger, more widespread, and more treelike, as shown by fossils of plants such as Calamites (below).

LEPIDODENDRON

Scale trees Lepidodendron were giant cousins of club mosses (above right). They grew spore-producing cones at the ends of their stems (above).

WHEN FERNS RULED

During the Carboniferous period, some ferns grew to large sizes in the warm, wet conditions. They were the size of the trees of today. They piled up in layers when they died and formed vast swamps. These layers became fossilized into black mineral rock we burn today as fuel—coal. There were also plant groups, similar to mosses and ferns, that once thrived around the world, such as seed ferns. However, they have since died out.

HOW MOSSES AND FERNS GROW

Mosses, liverworts, and ferns are plants. This means they do not eat food, as animals do. They get their food from minerals and light energy through a process called photosynthesis.

PLANT COLORS

Plants use various pigments to trap sunlight. Chlorophyll can be varying shades of green. Carotenes are mostly red or orange, while xanthophylls usually have a yellow color. Some plants have several of these pigments.

PLANT CELLS

Chloroplasts help carry out photosynthesis. They are the small green blobs next to the outer walls of plant cells.

CAPTURING LIGHT ENERGY

All plants live and grow using light energy, which they trap using substances called pigments. Most of these pigments, such as chlorophyll, are green. This is why most plants are green. The energy is used to combine water with carbon dioxide from the air. Then sugars are made as food for the plant.

CHLOROPLASTS

Photosynthesis occurs in chloroplasts. Within the double-layered outer membrane are grana (stacks) of disklike thylakoids floating in a fluid called the stroma.

Thylakoids contain the pigments.

SUNLIGHT

Stroma

Stromule
(connecting
bridge)

Thylakoid

Granum
(stack)

Outer membrane

Inner membrane

During photosynthesis, water is taken in from the soil and rain, or as vapor.

WATER FROM SOIL OR RAIN

FOOD (HIGH-ENERGY SUGARS)

Plants need carbon dioxide, which makes up only 0.003 percent of air.

CARBON DIOXIDE FROM AIR

OXYGEN RELEASED INTO AIR

GAS EXCHANGE

Plant leaves need to take in carbon dioxide and give out oxygen, a process known as gas exchange. This happens through tiny holes in the leaf surface known as stomata (right).

PHOTOSYNTHESIS

Plants use their high-energy food to build complicated body parts from minerals taken in from the plant's surroundings. The process of capturing light energy to make food is called photosynthesis, which means "building with light." It also makes oxygen as a waste product, which is released into the air.

OUR NEED FOR PLANTS

People and animals must take in oxygen to stay alive. Plants produce continuing supplies of oxygen through photosynthesis, which keeps oxygen in the air for us to breathe.

COLORED FRONDS

Some ferns and mosses are grown and bred by scientists for their unusual colors, such as red, brown, yellow, orange, and even blue. These decorative colors are caused not only by the colored pigments used for photosynthesis, but also by the pigments' breaking down as the fronds become older.

Cylosporus swamp ferns grow mainly in tropical and warmer southern regions. They have many color variations.

WHAT ARE MOSSES?

Mosses form the plant group Bryophtya. They are mostly small, low-growing green plants that thrive in damp places, such as shady woodlands.

SHADY AND DAMP

Many kinds of mosses need to stay damp or even soaking wet (above, inset). Unlike plants with long roots, they cannot take up water from deep in the ground. So their main types of habitats are damp and shady (above).

MAIN PARTS OF A MOSS

Most mosses have lots of small, green leaflets growing on short stems. They are held above rootlike rhizoids that secure them in place.

INSIDE A MOSS

Mosses have many microscopic cells, but they are not organized into groups of tubes called vascular bundles. However, some mosses have stiffer strands that stand up and carry some water.

NON-VASCULAR

Ferns and flowering plants have pipelike structures inside called vascular bundles. These bundles transport water and sap within the plant body. They are stiff, which helps the plant to grow tall. Mosses are non-vascular plants. They lack stiffened vessels and cannot grow very tall. Water and other fluids pass through the microscopic cells or along channels between them.

GRIMMIA

Grimmia (sea moss) *is unusual among mosses because it grows along the seashore. It can withstand a certain amount of salty water.*

GOBLIN'S GOLD

The moss *Schistostega pennata* is known as goblin's gold because of its glowing green appearance. It can survive in dimly lit places, such as rocky overhangs, caves, and animal burrow entrances. It glows in the gloom because it has clear microscopic cells like tiny lenses that focus light onto its chloroplasts. This leads to better photosynthesis.

Goblin's gold is also known as luminescent moss or glow moss.

LANCELEAF

Various types of moss are named after their leaflet shapes, like red lanceleaf moss and ruggedleaf moss, both types of Schlotheimia.

PINCUSHIONS

Some mosses grow in round clumps with the leaflets pointing outward, known as the pincushion habit.

ROOTS AND LEAVES

On the outside, a typical moss seems to have parts like those of a flowering plant, such as roots, stems, and leaves. But inside, the parts are much simpler in structure. The "roots" are rhizoids. Although they anchor the moss to its growing place, they do not take up water and minerals, as true roots do. Instead a moss takes in water and minerals all over its body. Moss leaves are known as leaflets.

FEATHERS

Feather moss Hylocomium, *named after its feathery shape, is common in conifer forests with plenty of surface water.*

15

LIVERWORT SHAPES

WEED PEST
The Lunularia liverwort grows as a weed on paths and in greenhouses. It varies in color, from bright green to faded yellow.

RHIZOIDS
A liverwort's rootlike rhizoids form a network that looks like tangled string.

OIL BODIES
A microscopic view of cells inside a liverwort shows rounded blobs known as oil bodies. They are a feature of liverworts, but how the plant uses them is not yet known.

ROOTLESS PLANTS

Like mosses, liverworts are fairly simple plants. They lack true roots to take in water and minerals. If they have vascular tubes to distribute water and sap around their bodies, the tubes are very simple. Liverworts rely on absorbing water and minerals from the surroundings through their body surfaces and passing them through their cells and tissues.

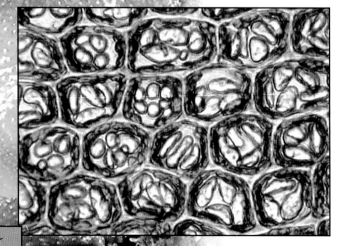

WINTER FOOD

Some liverworts are tough and can stand extreme cold. They grow far north into the Arctic region and high up on mountains, where most other plants cannot survive. Many animals in these places eat a mixture of liverworts, mosses, and lichens, especially in the winter. Such plant-eaters include caribou, musk oxen, Arctic hares, and lemmings.

Porella *(right)* and Scapania *(right, inset)* are leafy liverworts, having mosslike leaflets rather than a fleshy, lumpy body. Porella grows especially on tree bark, while Scapania *prefers rocky areas.*

PELLIA

Metzgaria *(right) can be grown in aquariums on rocks, wood, or in the water. It is popularly known as pellia.*

THALLUS

Most liverworts have a main body called the thallus that is flattened and round. In some types, it resembles the human liver, giving these plants their common name. Other liverworts have mosslike stems and leaflets.

RICCIA

Like pellia, riccia is found in ponds, lakes, slow rivers, and aquariums. A well-known species is Riccia fluitans, also called slender riccia or crystalwort.

Liverworts and mosses provide food under the snow for Arctic hares.

PELLIA

There are many kinds of pellia liverworts, but not all have the scientific name Pellia. Some are thallose liverworts (above), whose main body is lobed, flattened, or ribbon-shaped.

MOSS AND LIVERWORT HABITATS

There are about 10,000 species of mosses, and about the same number of liverworts. Most live in damp habitats.

DIM CORNERS

The hot sun is the enemy of many mosses and liverworts. They prefer cool, shaded places, such as behind barrels, where bricks, wood, and ground never become too dry.

WHICH SIDE OF THE WALL?
Mosses and liverworts grow much better on the shady side of a wall than on the sunny side.

CAVES
The dark insides of caves are ideal for liverworts, mosses, and other simple plants. Rainwater trickles in and keeps the air humid, helping to prevent these plants from drying out.

NATURAL HABITATS
Some of the best natural habitats for mosses and liverworts are in caves, on rocky overhangs, under boulders, and in deep cracks and crevices in rocks and fallen logs. These places usually lack soil and are too dark for other plants.

BIOCRUSTS

Specialized types of liverworts, mosses, lichens, and other plants form what is called a biocrust on soil in very dry regions. The crust is hard and lumpy, and can be up to 4 inches (10 cm) thick. Biocrusts are also known as biological crusts or macrobiotic crust layers. They prevent other plants from growing, forming bare-looking areas. But they also help the soil keep its moisture.

Biocrusts cover large areas in Utah.

EPIPHYTES AND SPRAY ZONES

Epiphytes are living things that grow on plants, using them for support. Epiphytic mosses and liverworts are especially common in rain forests (left), where they hang down from the large trees. They also thrive on rocks and boulders near streams, rapids, and waterfalls, where they receive soaking spray (below). Some very small types grow in tiny cracks in old wood (bottom).

ARTIFICIAL HABITATS

People have created many new kinds of habitats for mosses and liverworts. These include walls made of bricks and stones, untreated wood such as fences, sheds, and other buildings, and under tiles, slates, and other roofing materials. If minerals and nutrients are scarce, mosses and liverworts can go into a resting phase, then begin growing again when the food supply grows.

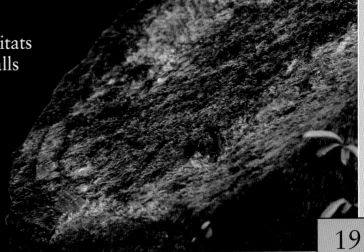

19

Mosses and liverworts may be simple plants in some ways. But their methods of reproduction are quite complicated.

TWO GENERATIONS

These plants have a two-stage life cycle, known as alternation of generations. The main moss plant grows from a spore and produces gametes, male and female sex cells. It is known as the gametophyte stage. In the second stage, a sporophyte grows on the gametophyte and produces the spores.

LIFE CYCLE

The main moss plant grows two types of gamete-producing structures at its upper ends. One makes male gametes—sperm cells. The other makes female gametes—egg cells.

FEMALE

Egg cells (below, central blue lump) are made in the archegonium. Sperm cells swim to it through the narrow part called the venter (right).

1. The antheridia at the tip of a male leaflet produce male gametes. Each has two tiny tails and swims to the female gametes.

2. The archegonium at the tip of a female leaflet makes female gametes. Male gametes swim to them in water drops.

MALE

The antheridia that produce a moss' sperm cells look like tiny flowers at the end of the leaflet (above left). Each antheridium (dark blue, sausage-shaped) has many sperm cells.

HAPLOID AND DIPLOID

The life cycle of a plant goes between the number of sets of DNA. Gametophytes have one set, called a haploid. In a sporophyte, two gametes join to make a double set, a diploid. Then the cycle repeats.

LIVERWORTS

As in mosses, liverworts have male and female parts that produce the sex cells (right). They may be on the same plant (dioecious) or different plants (monoecious).

3. At fertilization a male and female gamete join to form a zygote. This grows into the sporophyte with its stalked capsule.

Capsule

Operculum (cap)

3

Calyptra (capsule case)

Seta (stalk)

4

5

4. The capsule case falls away. In dry conditions the operculum then detaches so the spores can disperse.

5. If a spore lands somewhere suitable, it starts to germinate into a small, long, thin gametophyte stage called the protonema.

MOSS PROTONEMA

Moss plants begin as small rows or chains of cells (blue) growing out of their spore cases (brown). The protonema gradually develops into the main plant.

GEMMAE

In asexual reproduction, small cups form and release tiny clumps of cells, called gemmae, that grow into new plants. These plants are clones, meaning they have the same genes as the parent.

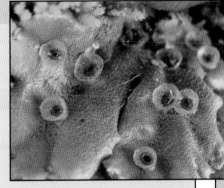

Gemma cups grow on the thallus (main body) of the liverwort Marchantia.

MOSS CAPSULES

A moss' stalked, spore-containing capsules are called sporangia. The spores are tiny specks inside the tough-walled container (below, purple) and are usually released in dry weather.

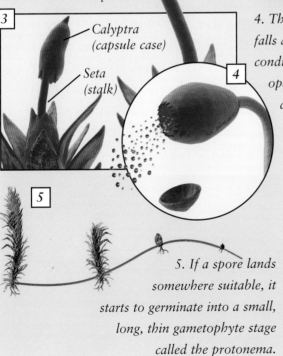

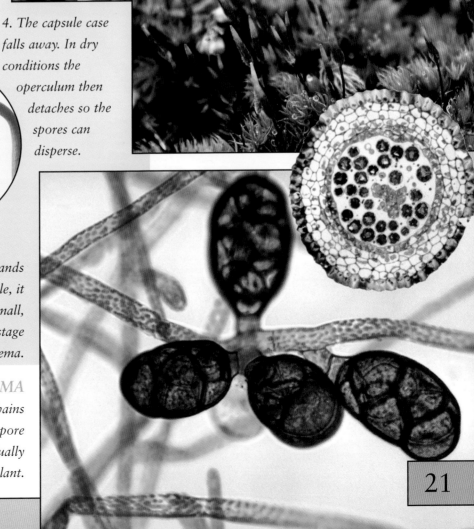

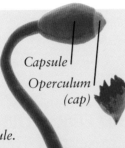

21

HORNWORTS

Hornworts, which make up the plant group Anthocerophyta, resemble mosses and liverworts in many ways. They are small, green, and often unnoticed.

HORNWORT SPOROPHYTES

The parts of a hornwort that release the spores are usually long and thin with pointed ends. They often resemble the horns of antelopes and similar animals, which is how these plants got their common name.

YELLOW SPORES

Phaeoceros *hornworts produce yellow spores from horn-shaped capsules. Some kinds grow along the seashore, but most are found in woodlands, along ditches, and among crops in farm fields.*

NEED FOR MOISTURE

Like mosses and liverworts, hornworts are non-vascular. They do not have tubelike vessels inside, and they lack true roots or leaves. They absorb water and minerals through their entire body surface. Hornworts live in damp, shady places. About 150 species of hornworts are known.

SPORES TO GO

The spore capsule, called the sporangium, of Dendroceros *(tree horn) splits open to release its spores. This hornwort grows mainly on trees in tropical regions.*

ELATERS

Some hornworts and liverworts have spiral or twisted parts called elaters inside the spore capsule. These untwist as they dry out, releasing the spores so they catch the wind and spread more widely.

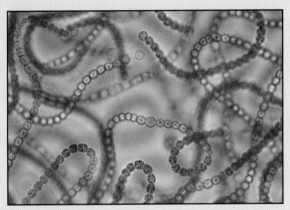
FOREST OF CAPSULES

The long, thin sporophyte capsules of Anthoceros *release dark-brown or black spores. As in liverworts and mosses, they grow up from the archegonia, the female gametes on the thallus, after fertilization by male gametes.*

TWO LIFE STAGES

Hornworts have a two-stage life cycle like those of mosses and liverworts. The thallus is the gametophyte. It has one set of DNA, making it a haploid. The sporophyte stages that release the spores grow on it like small parasites. These sporophytes are diploid, having a double set of DNA.

THALLUS TYPES

Some hornworts are round, while others grow as ribbons or straps with a central "rib" and wavy edges. Some, such as Dendroceros, *split or branch off.*

23

FERNS AND FRONDS

Ferns make up the group Pteridophyta, also known as Filicophyta. These plants, most of which are green, vary in size from smaller than a fingernail to as tall as trees.

BLADE

The biggest, greenest part of a fern is its blade (lamina), which is a leaf with many divided parts.

STIPE

The tall, stiffened stalk or stem that holds up the blade is known as the stipe.

RHIZOME

The rhizome is a creeping form of the stem that grows horizontally under the ground.

ROOTS

Fern roots are similar to the roots of flowering plants. They are tough and strong, holding the fern firmly in the ground. Their tiny hairs absorb water and minerals.

RACHIS

In the blade, the rachis is the stiff, stemlike part from which pinnae grow.

PINNA

A pinna is one main part of the blade. Pinnae often grow in pairs, one on each side of the rachis.

PINNULE

Each pinna may be branched into smaller parts known as pinnules.

VESSELS

A cut-through fern stem shows the vessel bundles, known as the vascular system. These include phloem tubes (blue) for nutrient-rich sap and stiffer xylem (inner circles) for water and dissolved minerals.

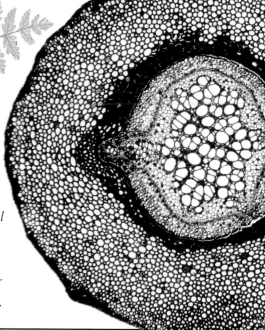

*Fern fronds grow by unrolling
from a tight bundle known as
the crozier or fiddlehead (left).
This resembles the peg end of
a fiddle or violin (below).*

FAST GROWERS

*In good conditions, ferns
such as brackens can spread
quickly and carpet the
ground in a few weeks.
Many ferns like shady
places, such as under trees.*

STEMS

*The stipes of
tree ferns, such as
Cibotium, are thick and
woody. They form a treelike
trunk that helps the plant stay
upright. These plants can grow
up to 20 feet (6 m) tall.*

VASCULAR PLANTS

Ferns are the simplest types of tracheo-phytes (vascular plants). They have parts inside called vascular bundles that carry liquids and nutrient-containing sap from one part to another. Flowering plants are also vascular and more complex than non-vascular mosses and liverworts.

GROWING TALL

The tubelike vessels in a fern's stipe are often strengthened with stiff, woody substances. This allows the stem to grow long and tall without bending or buckling. A fern also has true roots that anchor it in the soil and take in water and minerals for growth. These two features are further differences between ferns and mosses.

STOLONS

Some ferns have stolons, also called runners, which are stems that grow sideways, usually along the surface of the soil. At places called nodes that are found along the stolon, new roots and upright stems grow. Stolons help ferns to spread outward in a form of asexual reproduction.

New fronds grow from a Boston fern (Nephrolepis) stolon.

25

WHERE FERNS GROW

There are about 20,000 species of ferns around the world. Most are small and grow in damp places, but some can thrive in deserts.

FOREST FERNS
Many hundreds of species of ferns are found among various areas with trees—from cool, broad-leaved woods (above) to conifer forests and tropical rain forests.

DAMP AND SHADE
Ferns grow in almost all habitats, including mountaintops, forests, rivers, lakes, and swamps. But ferns do not grow in the ocean. Most species are found in damp places with plenty of rain and shade from the sun, such as in rain forests. Many species do not need light, so they can be found along the bottoms of valleys.

MOUNTAIN FERNS
Sadleria is a small tree fern found in rocky areas in Hawaii. It is popular as a decorative fern indoors, in gardens, and in rock gardens.

AZOLLA

Azolla, known as mosquito fern or fairy moss, is a tiny fern that grows in water. It is sometimes mistaken for duckweed *Lemna*, which is a flowering plant. *Azolla* has very small, simple fronds that look like overlapping scales.

Azolla (inset) can become a terrible pest, choking waterways with its thick growth.

PIONEER PLANTS

Ferns are sometimes known as pioneer plants. This means they are the first plants to grow in an area that has gone through some kind of great change, such as a wildfire, flood, or earthquake. Fern spores are tiny and are constantly blowing in the wind. They are likely to land on bare soil found in changed habitats and spring up quickly.

EPIPHYTIC FERNS

Some stag's horn ferns, Platycerium (below), are epiphytic. They grow on other plants, including trees, using them for support. They are not parasites because they do not take nutrients from their host plant.

RIVERSIDE FERNS

Ferns, such as tree ferns in New Zealand (below), are especially suited for growing alongside rivers, streams, lakes, and irrigation canals.

DRY FERNS

Rock-cap ferns, Polypodium (above), are specialized for dry, stony habitats. Their many small roots grip the rock and search for precious water.

27

FROND SHAPES

GLADE FERNS
The Diplazium *blade fern has long blades with jagged edges.*

Most ferns are identified by the shape of the frond, which includes the stipe and the lamina.

DIGIT FERNS
Some types of Doryopteris *(left) are known as digit ferns because the blade is divided into five parts, like the digits (fingers) of a hand.*

BRANCHING PATTERNS
Most ferns have one leaf on each stem. Each leaf, called a blade, is divided into the pinnae. Pinnae that are divided into pinnules are known as twice-cut. Some species are thrice-cut, meaning the pinnules are split into even smaller parts—pinnulets.

ELKHORN FERNS
Platycerium *ferns (right) are known as stag's horns or elkhorns because of their flat surfaces, which look like the antlers of a stag or elk. They are popular decorative plants in gardens and houses.*

LACE FERNS
Each blade of a Sphenomeris *(left) is cut three times. This shape led to such common names for the plant as lace fern and parsley fern.*

CROCODILE FERNS
Microsorium *ferns include crocodile ferns (left) and Java ferns. They are often grown in aquariums.*

MAIDENHAIR FERN

There are more than 200 species of Adiantum (maidenhair ferns), including the delta maidenhair (left). Some grow naturally on rocks and cliffs near waterfalls. They also grow on damp stone walls.

SILVER FERN

One of the best known ferns is the silver fern. This New Zealand tree fern is known scientifically as *Cyathea dealbata*. Its common names include ponga and kaponga. The fronds have a shiny, silvery underside.

The silvery white color of Cyathea dealbata sets it apart from other ferns.

CLOVER FERN

Marsilea quadrifolia *(right) is named for its similarity to the four-leaved clover. It grows in ponds and rivers and is used for scientific research.*

UNCUT FERNS

Some ferns have uncut blades with smooth or wavy edges, like the leaves of many flowering plants. These blades can be circular, long and thin, or shaped like a heart or a dagger.

TONGUE FERNS

More than 700 species of Elaphoglossum *exist around the world. Some are called tongue ferns because of their blade shape, which is known as simple or uncut.*

29

Ferns are found on every continent except Antarctica. They are some of the toughest survivors, even in icy regions.

LOW TEMPERATURES

Some ferns can withstand months of freezing weather. The fern *Cystopteris fragilis* is found well into the Arctic region. It is named after its stipe, which tends to snap easily.

LONG TONGUE

Ophioglossum vulgatum *(left) is known as adder's tongue because its spore capsule resembles a snake's flicking tongue.*

FERN SCREEN

Planted ferns can grow into dense hedgerows or screens. These shield the view or shelter other, less hardy plants, such as in a flower bed.

LITTLE AND LARGE

The kidney fern Trichomanes reniforme *(left) from New Zealand has fronds less than 4 inches (10 cm) tall. The giant mule's-foot or king fern, Angiopteris evecta (above), has fronds reaching 20 feet (6 m) in length.*

Osmunda regalis thrives in marshes and bogs. It is used as a central structure in wetland gardens.

TALL AS TREES

The biggest species of ferns are the tree ferns in the group Cyatheales. Some reach heights of 80 feet (25 m). Certain species have adapted to cold habitats. Others live in dry, rocky places where broad-leaved and conifer trees suffer from thin soil and a lack of water.

TREE FERNS

Stands of tree ferns form "fern woodlands" in areas of New Zealand, Australia, East Asia, and South America.

FIRST TO GROW

Ferns are often the first plants to grow on new land, such as land formed by cooled, hardened volcanic lava. They get by with little soil or water, being able to survive periods of poor nutrients and drought better than flowering plants. After the rapid growth of ferns, other plants eventually take over.

Asian swordfern, Nephrolepsis multiflora, grows on new lava rocks in Hawaii.

GOLDEN POLYPODY

Epiphytic Phlebodium aureum *(left), also known as serpent fern, is found in the warmer, eastern regions of North and South America. Its fronds are up to 4.3 feet (1.3 m) in length.*

GRAPE FERN

Some Botrychium *ferns are named after their spore capsules, which resemble bunches of grapes (right). Others are known as moonworts. Various species are found across North America, Europe, and Asia.*

HOW FERNS REPRODUCE

The main fern plant stage—the sporophyte—has two sets of DNA (diploid). The other stage, the gametophyte, has only one set of DNA (haploid) and is much smaller.

1. Hundreds of tiny, tough, lightweight spores form by cell division inside the sporangium, the spore capsule.

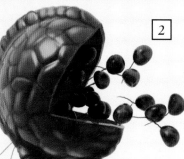

2. The spore capsule usually opens in dry weather. This is when conditions are best for the spores to spread long distances.

SORI SHAPES

Sporangia are grouped in clusters, called sori, of various shapes on the underside of the blade. They form dark stripes in bird's nest fern, Asplenium nidus (above), large rusty patches in Asplenium adiantum-nigrum (above right), lumps at the leaflet tips in the climbing fern Lygodium (below left), and strips along the edges in the mule's-foot fern Angiopteris (background).

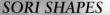

Like mosses and liverworts, ferns have two stages in the alternation of generations. In ferns the sporophyte, the spore-making stage, forms the main plant, rather than the gametophyte stage as in mosses.

FERTILE AND STERILE FRONDS

Fronds that bear spores are called sporophylls. Other fronds, trophophylls, are sterile and do not make spores. In some ferns, these two frond types are similar. In other ferns, such as the cinnamon fern, they look different. Its fertile fronds are small and yellow-brown, while the sterile ones are larger and green.

Cinnamon fern, Osmundastrum cinnamomeum

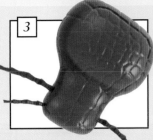

3. If a spore lands in a suitable place, it germinates into the next stage, the small green prothallus.

4. The prothallus grows to become heart-shaped or kidney-shaped. It is usually smaller than a fingernail.

6. An egg and sperm join at fertilization to form a zygote. This sends up a shoot that is the start of the new fern plant.

5. The prothallus grows gamete-producing parts—antheridia for sperm cells and archegonia for egg cells.

INDUSIA

Some groups of sori have umbrella-shaped structures called indusia. These shrivel away or flip back to release the spores.

SEXUAL REPRODUCTION

Unlike asexual reproduction, sexual reproduction by male and female gametes involves exchanging DNA. That means offspring plants have different combinations of genes than the parents do, which can help them to adapt to new conditions.

PROTHALLUS

The prothallus, such as that of Dicksonia antarctica, is green and can go through photosynthesis like the main fern plant.

DRIED OUT

Spore capsules are usually on the undersides of the leaf blades. In some, like Pteridium, the capsule (above, blue and white) dries out and splits open. This shoots the spores (brown) out into the wind.

33

CLUB MOSSES

T he club mosses, Lycopodophyta, belong to an ancient plant group that long ago was much bigger and far more widespread than today.

PREHISTORIC GIANTS

There are about 1,000 living species of club mosses. They are a small remainder of the massive species that lived long ago. During the Carboniferous period, they towered to heights of more than 130 feet (40 m) and formed vast swampy forests with huge ferns and other non-flowering plants.

BOG CLUB MOSS

Species of Lycopodiella *are called bog club mosses because of their habitat, although some like rocky places.*

BRIGHT GREEN

Huperzia lucidula *of North America is known as the shining club moss because of its bright green color.*

MARSHY HABITATS

The marsh club moss Lycopodiella inundata *can survive being flooded for long periods. It spreads by strand-like stolons (stems).*

CLUBBED ENDS

Spore capsules of many species, such as the interrupted club moss Lycopodiella annotinum, *are lumpy or club-shaped, giving them the name club moss.*

SHARP LEAVES

Species in the Huperzia *group, including the daggerleaf club moss (above), are widespread across northern and tropical*

DWARF SPECIES

Selaginella arbuscula *is the dwarf spikemoss, a tropical species from the Pacific islands that can be grown as a houseplant.*

SPIKEMOSS

One of the largest club moss groups is Selaginella, *often called spikemosses, with more than 500 species.*

GROWING TALL

Some club mosses may look like large mosses. But they are vascular plants, like ferns. Their internal vessels are strengthened with woody fibers and can grow to more than 7 feet (2 m). Also like ferns, they reproduce using spores.

STROBILI

Certain club mosses produce spores in strobili, structures similar to the cones of conifer trees. Megaspores grow into female gametophyte plants, and microspores into male ones.

RESURRECTION MOSS

Species of resurrection plants include the club moss Selaginella tamariscina *(above) and* Polypodium *ferns. They fade when dry and turn bright green when wet.*

QUILLWORTS

The group Isoetales is often called the quillworts group. Some experts include them with club mosses, while others think they are only closely related. Their leaves grow from a central base and are long, thin, and hollow, like an old-fashioned quill pen. There are about 150 species of quillworts, most growing in water or very wet places.

Appalachian quillworts often grow near water.

HORSETAILS

Bottlebrush, mare's tail, snake grass, scouring rush—these are names for various horsetails, which form the group Sphenophyta (Equisetophyta).

ANCIENT TIMES

Horsetails are vascular plants that reproduce by spores. They have many similarities to ferns. The first kinds appeared more than 350 million years ago. The group became very widespread, and some were huge, up to 100 feet (30 m) in height.

PIONEERS

Horsestails, like ferns, grow quickly on disturbed ground, including a gardener's freshly dug flower borders.

HOLLOW STEM

Horsetails such as the water horsetail, Equisetum fluviatile, *have a hollow, tubelike stem. The small black points are whorls of tiny leaves.*

LEAFY CIRCLE

Leaves on horsetails grow in circles from a part of the stem called the node. Then there is a gap, the internode, before the next circle. These stems usually have vertical ridges.

WOOD HORSETAILS

Horsetails sometimes take over the shaded ground under trees and form a dense thicket where other plants cannot grow.

USEFUL HORSETAILS

Horsetail stems contain tiny grains of the mineral silica, which also forms sand. They were once collected and used for rubbing, scouring, and polishing, like a natural type of sandpaper.

SMALL SURVIVORS

There are about 15 living species of horsetails, all in the genus *Equisetum*. Most have green, upright stems that carry out photosynthesis like a leaf. Narrow, spiky leaves grow in circles at intervals along the stem, like the ribs of an umbrella. The branching roots go deep into the soil, which means the plant can take up water from far below the surface, even during dry periods.

WHISK FERNS

Whisk ferns are close relatives of true ferns. They form a very small group, Psilophyta, with a few species in the genus *Psilotum*. They are vascular plants but with a simple structure. The leaflike parts are known as enations, while the "roots" are rhizoids, similar to those of mosses.

Whisk ferns make spores in the stem tips (inset), each with three sporangia.

PROBLEM MOSSES AND FERNS

The deep roots of a horsetail (right) make removing these plants a problem. Even if pulled up, bits of the root left behind can grow into new plants.

CLIMBING FERNS

The Japanese climbing fern Lygodium japonica *(above) has become a major pest in many areas. Its vinelike growths can be 100 feet (30 m) long.*

Weeds are plants growing where they are not wanted. Ferns, mosses, and liverworts are sometimes seen as weeds.

BRACKEN

The bracken fern (above) is poisonous to some animals, like cattle (inset). It is difficult to kill the plant with chemicals, so it has to be crushed or burned to stop it from spreading.

INVASIVE SPECIES
In their natural habitats, plants usually do not overrun their environments. Animals eat them, and microbes cause plant-killing diseases. In a new habitat, there may be no such control. A plant can multiply unchecked as an invasive species and take over the area.

UNWANTED GUESTS
Brackens, *Pteridium*, are among the worst fern weeds. They spread by rhizomes and quickly crowd out other plants. Other problem species include climbing ferns *Lygodium*, Kraus' club moss, field horsetails, and heath star moss *Campylopus introflexus*.

MARCHANTIA

The liverworts Marchantia *(left) and* Lunularia *can be pests in gardens, greenhouses, and plant nurseries.*

HEATH STAR MOSS

Introduced to Europe from the Southern Hemisphere in the 1940s, Campylopus introflexus (right) reached North America in the 1970s. This invasive species greatly affects desert habitats.

GIANT SALVINIA—A GROWING THREAT

The floating freshwater fern called giant salvinia, *Salvinia molesta*, grows rapidly and multiplies asexually when small pieces break off the main body and grow into new plants. Originally from South America, it first appeared in the U.S. in the 1990s. A few years later, it became a pest in many southern states. It covers the water's surface and endangers fish and other water life.

Giant salvinia fronds (left) form thick green mats (below). The salvinia weevil (right) eats the weed and can help control outbreaks.

PRETTY MOSSES AND FERNS

HANGING BASKET

Epiphytic ferns and mosses that grow on trees also thrive in hanging baskets with little soil and occasional watering.

MOSS GARDEN

Moss that grows heavily in an area can form a "carpet" across the ground.

Various kinds of mosses, ferns, and liverworts are prized for their beauty and use in decorating. Some are grown and studied in scientific research.

LANDSCAPING

Dozens of species of ferns and mosses are bred to enhance their unusual colors. The colors set them apart from each other and from other landscape features, such as walls and steps.

IN THE BACKGROUND

Certain types of lacy mosses and tall tree ferns are impressive on their own. Other species are grown to provide green backdrops for colorful flowers, which stand out even more against a duller green background. Mosses and ferns also "soften" hard features in gardens and parks, such as rock gardens, river banks, and stone walls.

ENDANGERED FERNS

The rare fern *Marsilea villosa* is known in its home region of Hawaii as *ihi'ihi*. It only grows in a few lowland areas that are flooded regularly by seasonal rains. This species needs plenty of water to complete its life cycle and release spores. It then needs dry ground to grow into healthy plants. Conservation measures include removing grazing cattle and invasive plants.

Marsilea villosa *looks like a four-leaved clover.*

MOSS AND FERN FANS

People may be intrigued by the long history of mosses, ferns, and their relatives. They like the idea of having a plant display that could almost date from the time of the dinosaurs. Also, certain species make great houseplants. They are grown in specially designed containers known as mosseries, ferneries, or terrariums. Some are used for seasonal traditions. In some regions, club mosses are used for Christmas decorations, such as wreaths.

PRIZED HUES
Unusual colors are sought after by plant growers. They breed certain plants to make the hues brighter and stronger, a practice known as selective breeding. Such species include painted ferns Athyrium *(above left), amau* Sadleria cyatheoides *(above right) and brakes* Pteris *(right).*

41

USEFUL MOSSES AND FERNS

Mosses, liverworts, and ferns have been used for many things around the house and garden, as food, as medicinal treatments, and even in industrial processes.

TREATING ILLNESS

Before scientific medicine, horsetails were used to stop bleeding. Liverworts were once used to treat liver problems such as jaundice because their thallus shapes resemble that part of the body.

FIDDLEHEAD FOOD

The soft, uncurling fronds of fiddlehead ferns can be boiled or steamed for eating.

SPHAGNUM

The moss Sphagnum soaks up water well, yet dries to become soft and springy. It has been used as a natural sponge for cleaning and also as a stuffing for mattresses and pillows.

DISAPPEARING LOGS

Tree fern logs are used as supports to grow epiphyte plants such as orchid flowers. But many tree ferns grow very slowly, less than 1 inch (2.5 cm) each year. In some areas, they are disappearing quickly.

STAG'S HORN CLUB MOSS

The club moss (ground pine) Lycopodium
clavatum *(above) produces tiny, pale,
powdery spores that have many uses.*

LYCOPODIUM POWDER

Spore powder from Lycopodium *can be
used in fireworks at concerts (above).*

SPORE DUST

*Fern and clubmoss spores
are extremely small, fine
particles. They have been
used for dusting fingerprints
(above) and also as a pore-
filler to smooth and seal
wooden items, such as
guitars and violins (right).*

PEAT AND FERTILIZER

Peat is nutrient-rich and used widely for
planting and improving soils in pots,
parks, and gardens. It consists of partially
decayed plant material of various kinds,
including mosses from marshes, bogs, and
other wetlands. In many areas, it is dug
up and bagged for sale at garden centers
and greenhouses. However, this destroys
the plants' specialized habitats.

THE WARDIAN CASE

In the 1820s, English doctor
Nathaniel Ward developed a
small glass case for growing,
protecting, and transporting
ferns and other plants. Before
this time, rare plants were
difficult to transport from
their remote homelands to
the gardens of Europe
and North America. The
Wardian case, a kind of
mini-greenhouse, allowed
plants to be collected
around the world.

*Nathaniel Ward (1791–
1868) and one type of
Wardian case (inset)*

CLASSIFICATION OF LIFE

Scientists classify living things depending on how their features and the parts inside them compare with those of other living things. In microscopic life-forms that have one cell each, these parts are very tiny. But they are important, because many of them are found in the cells of much larger living things, such as plants and animals. Single-celled bacteria and other microbes give us clues about how life on Earth started billions of years ago.

The main groups of living things are known as domains. The smaller groups that follow are usually kingdom, phylum (division), class, order, family, genus, and species. To see how this system works, follow the example on page 45 of how the fern *Polypodium formosanum* is classified in the Eukaria domain.

THE DOMAINS OF LIFE

BACTERIA

 Single-celled prokaryotes, found in most places on Earth

ARCHAEA

 Single-celled prokaryotes, many surviving in extreme conditions

EUKARYA

KINGDOMS

 PROTISTA: Single-celled eukaryotes, with some simple multicelled forms

 FUNGI: Multicelled life-forms that digest their food externally

 PLANTAE: Multicelled life-forms that obtain energy by photosynthesis

 ANIMALIA: Multicelled life-forms that get their energy by taking in food

GROUPS OF FERNS

Experts classify one of the main orders, or subgroups, of ferns—the Pteridopsida—into between six and 10 smaller groups, based on the features they share.

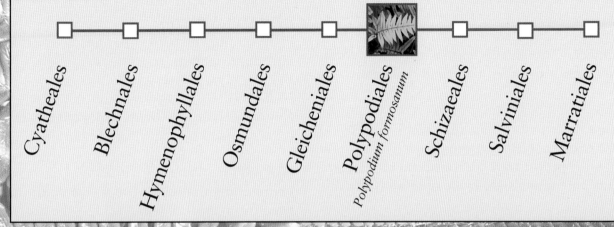

Cyatheales

Blechnales

Hymenophyllales

Osmundales

Gleicheniales

Polypodiales
Polypodium formosanum

Schizaeales

Salviniales

Marratiales

Polypodium formosanum originally came from East Asia. It is a popular plant in houses, conservatories, and greenhouses.

DOMAIN: Eukarya

KINGDOM: Plantae

DIVISION: Pteridophyta

CLASS: Pteridopsida

ORDER: Polypodiales

FAMILY: Polypodiaceae

GENUS: *Polypodium*

SPECIES: *formosanum*

Polypodium formosanum (green caterpillar fern)

GLOSSARY

ASEXUAL REPRODUCTION
Reproduction in which offspring have the same genes as the parents

BLADE
Large, green, leaflike part of a fern that may be divided into smaller parts known as pinnae or leaflets; also called the frond or lamina

CELL
Tiniest basic unit or "building block" of life; some microscopic living things, such as bacteria and most protists, are just one cell each; larger plants and animals are made of billions of cells

CELL MEMBRANE
Thin covering or "skin" of a living cell

CHLOROPHYLL
Green pigment that captures light energy to carry out photosynthesis

CHLOROPLAST
Tiny part inside a living cell that contains the substances needed to capture light energy and carry out photosynthesis

DIPLOID
Having two complete sets of DNA

DNA
Deoxyribonucleic acid, the chemical substance that carries genetic information about how a living thing grows and survives

EPIPHYTE
Living thing that grows on a plant, using it for physical support, but not taking nourishment from it as a parasite would

GAMETES
Single cells involved in sexual reproduction; male gametes are called sperm, and female gametes are called eggs

GERMINATE
When a plant seed, spore, or similar part starts to grow after reaching good conditions of light, moisture, and nutrients

HAPLOID
Having one complete set of DNA

INVASIVE SPECIES
Plant or animal species that has been artificially introduced into an ecosystem

NUCLEUS
Control center of a living cell; contains DNA and is surrounded by a nuclear membrane

PARASITE
Living thing that gains food, shelter, or other need from another living thing—the host—and in the process harms the host

PHOTOSYNTHESIS
Capturing light energy to join simple substances and create food, which is used by plants to grow, develop, and carry out life processes

PINNA
One of the main parts of a fern blade; also called a leaflet

PINNULE
One of the main parts of a fern pinna; also called a subleaflet

PROTHALLUS
Stage in the life cycle of ferns and other plants; at this stage, the plant is usually small, green, and heart-shaped; it produces the parts that make the gametes (sex cells)

RHIZOIDS
Rootlike parts of plants, such as mosses, that anchor the plant to the soil; they do not take up water and minerals like true roots

RHIZOME
Creeping form of a stem that grows horizontally, usually under the ground

SEXUAL REPRODUCTION
Reproduction that involves exchanging or mixing DNA, usually that of a female and male, so the offspring have genes that differ from those of their parents

STIPE
Tall, stiffened stalk or stem that holds up the blade of a fern

SPORES
Microscopic plant cells, each in a tough casing, that develop into new plants; spores are commonly made through asexual reproduction and, unlike seeds, do not store food

SPOROPHYTE
Stage in the life cycle of some plants and other living things that produces the spores

SYMBIOSIS
When two species exist closely together; both benefit from the partnership

THALLUS
Main body of a simple plant such as a liverwort

VASCULAR BUNDLES
Groups of specialized pipelike structures inside some species of plants; they transport water, sap, and other fluids within the plant body

Look for all the books in this series:

Cocci, Spirilla & Other Bacteria
Ferns, Mosses & Other Spore-Producing Plants
Molds, Mushrooms & Other Fungi
Protozoans, Algae & Other Protists
Redwoods, Hemlocks & Other
   Cone-Bearing Plants
Sunflowers, Magnolia Trees & Other
   Flowering Plants

FURTHER RESOURCES

FURTHER READING
Burnie, David. *Plant*. New York: DK Publishing, 2006.

Loves, June. *Ferns*. Philadelphia: Chelsea ClubHouse, 2005.

Spilsbury, Louise, and Richard Spilsbury. *How Do Plants Grow?* Chicago: Heinemann Library, 2006.

Stewart, Melissa. *Classification of Life*. Minneapolis: Twenty-First Century Books, 2008.

INTERNET SITES
FactHound offers a safe, fun way to find Internet sites related to this book. All of the sites on FactHound have been researched by our staff.

Here's all you do:
Visit *www.facthound.com*
FactHound will fetch the best sites for you!

INDEX